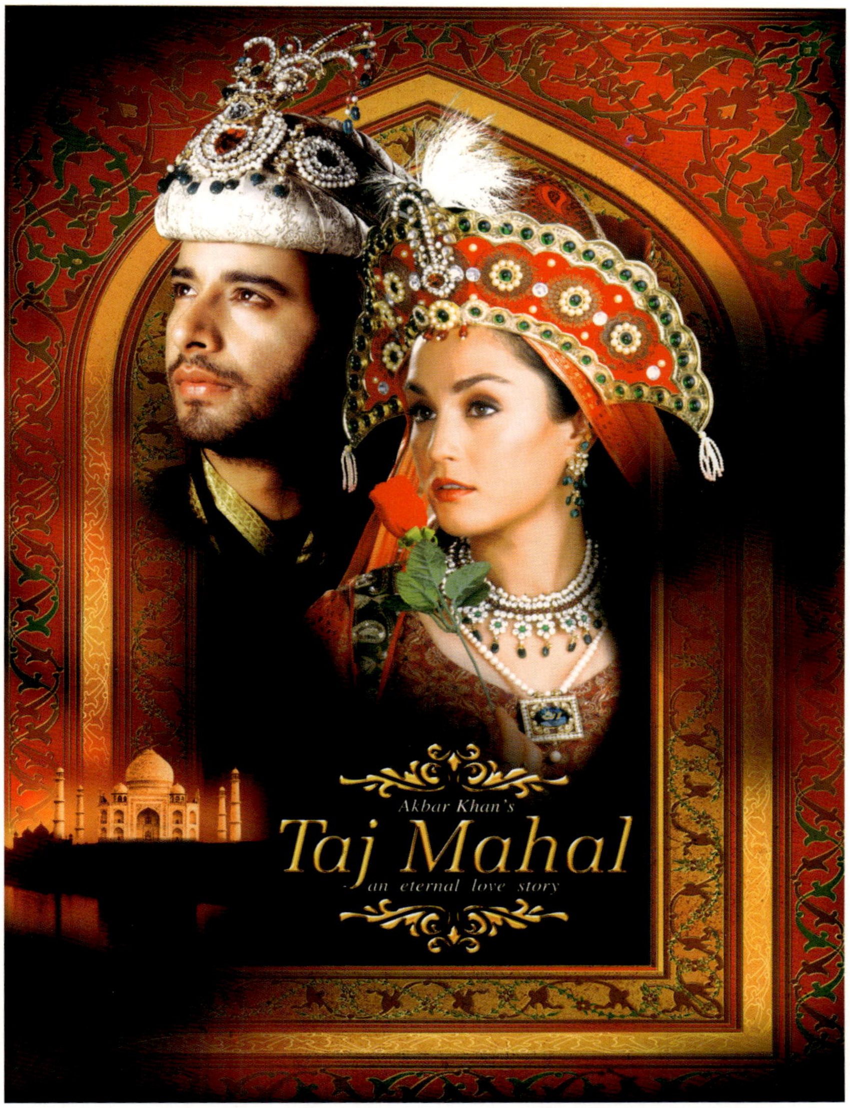

Making *of a* Motion Picture

by Suresh Kohli

OM
Om Books International

First Published in 2006 by
Om Books International
4379/4B Prakash House, Ansari Road, Darya Ganj, New Delhi 110 002, India.

Tel: 0091-11-2326 3363 / 2326 5303 Fax: 0091-11-2327 8091
sales@ombooks.com
www.ombooks.com

Photo Credits *(page 6, 7 & 9)* - Raghu Rai
Design & Layout - Ravi Gurnani @ Format / New Delhi

ISBN: 8187107448

1666

Contents

In memoriam
Emperor Shahjehan, 1592-1666

who immortalised love through a glorious monument
and inspired me to recreate Taj Mahal

Akbar Khan

To my Late mother Bibi Fatima Begum
who gave me life and instilled in it
the spirit of an Arabic prayer

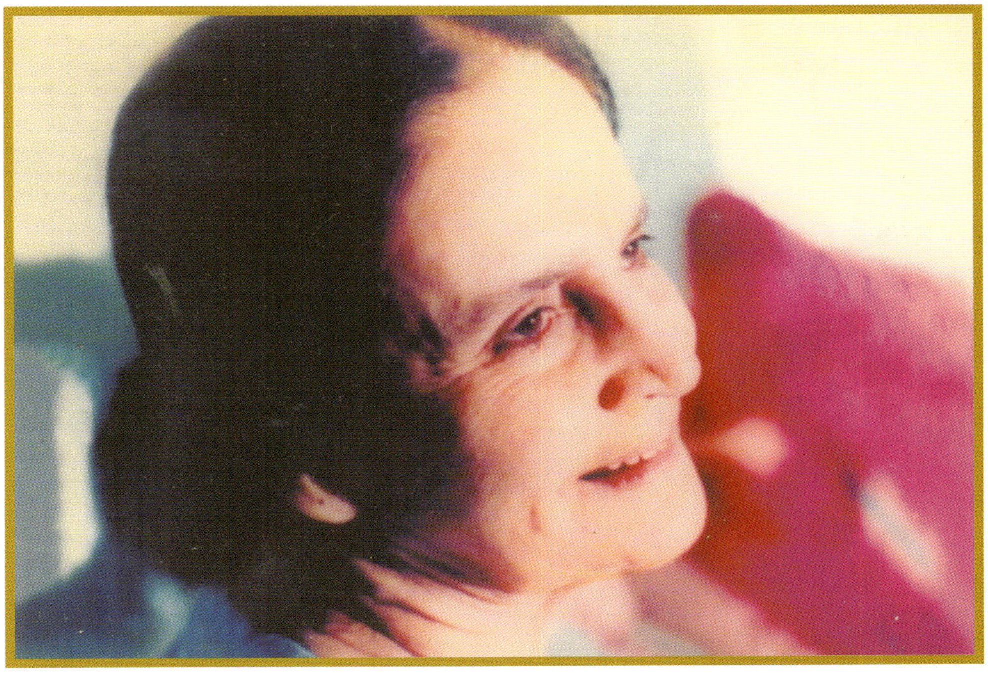

O Lord

Take not away my happiness, when you give me prosperity;
When you give me strength, take not away my sagacity;
When you give me glory, take not away my humility;
When you give me humility, take not away my dignity,
And take not away my grace, when you give me authority

May her soul rest in Peace - Amin!

Akbar Khan

been the original resting place of the beautiful empress who had been temporarily buried in a grave in Burhanpur, and had been shifted to the present site from the *supurdargah* after the marvellous monument was ready. *Taj Mahal* wasn't supposed to be Shahjehan's own burial place. Where now the two graves stand witness to the bygone era, only one of Mumtaz had been set up. Recorded history indicates that the emperor remained in mourning for two years, distancing himself from royal splendour, and took to wearing only white robes.

THE ARTISTS, the technicians, the light men and the spot boys stared bewildered at producer-director Akbar Khan, while he examined and supervised every little detail, and fussed over the absence of some continuity. One witnessed some of it on a set in Mumbai, and during several outdoor stints under the desert covered skies of Jodhpur, Jaipur, and Udaipur in Rajasthan, where a part of the theme song leading towards the climax was picturised on Kabir Bedi, apart from sequences featuring the legendary royal lovers. "He does not want to leave anything to anyone else's judgment," grumbled ace cameraman RM Rao, a veteran of numerous commercials doing his first feature film, and then he justified it in the same breath, saying, "he is trying to give birth to a dream." Rightly so, one assumes. "This is my future, and that of my family," whispered Akbar Khan, while discussing the intricacies of footwork involved in the picturising of a song with choreographer diva Saroj Khan. He grew up relishing a staple diet of Hollywood classics, like *Benhur*, *Elcid* and *Ten Commandments*, amongst others. Newcomers Zulfikar and Sonya listened attentively. Music maestro Naushad, the composer of almost all the classical and historical Hindi hits, returns to the big screen after a 14-year hiatus to try and recreate the atmosphere of a bygone era known for its patronage of music and musicians.

APART FROM the visual splendour, the film, perhaps, for the first time seeks to present the actual story of the Shahjehan-Mumtaz Mahal romance as it blossomed, and threatened to jolt Emperor Jahangir's scale of justice. It also seeks to portray the beginning of the sun setting on the Moghul empire. The extravaganza opens with the scene of a troubled old emperor being informed about the defeat of his eldest son and heir-apparent Dara Shikho at the hands of the defiant youngest Prince Aurangzeb. And as a gesture of the acceptance of his own defeat in the process, in reluctant salutation to the new king and as a measure of reconciliation, he requests daughter Jahanara to present the royal sword to the victorious. And then using the convenient but potent device of a series of flashbacks the unique love story starts to unfold. Every sequence showing the progress, the blossoming love, is a delight to watch. The outdoor locations, particularly a song picturised in some never before seen Kashmir location is breathtaking. The grandeur of the Taj Mahal, the monument, and that of the film can only be experienced and not described. The miniscule postcard size picture clicked in front of the structure fails to give out the truth about its overall size, its imposing slender minarets, each of the 133-feet high towers, the 70'x 120' dome that covers the centre of the building decorated with inlaid floral patterns and passages from the holy *Quran*. The actual scale of the architecture, designed by a Turk, is awesome as, indeed, is the immortal love story. More so the tragic end. The old dethroned imprisoned emperor can helplessly watch, the marvel built in the memory of his beloved, only from a distance.

THE VIEWERS' hearts are bound to reach out to Kabir Bedi, who effortlessly essays the role of the tired old Shahjehan, in Akbar Khan's celluloid interpretation of the ageless love story. Sonya Jehan, the granddaughter of the legendary singing star Noorjehan, who migrated to Pakistan after the Partition, plays Mumtaz Mahal, while model Zulfikar acts out the role of the young Shahjehan with conviction. A surprise is Manisha Koirala in the role of Jahanara, the emperor's favourite daughter, who's also his sole companion during the seven years of exile. The surprise of surprises, according to editor Sanjay Varma, is Pooja Batra as the ambitious, arrogant, scheming Empress Noorjehan. Aurangzeb's character by Arabaaz Khan makes for a worthy performance that lifts the tensions in the sequences featuring him. Arbaaz Ali, son of the late hero-turned-character actor-turned villain Ajit, portrays Emperor Jahangir with finesse and elegance. Even the lesser characters justify the maker's choice as they do stand out. Lyrics by Naqsh Lyallpuri and Gulrez Syed, dialogue by Rajiv Mirza, Muhafiz Haider and Gulrez Syed and art direction by Chandrakant More are other important credits, as also the massive action sequences by Sham Kaushal. The gorgeous dresses, headgears, crowns by Anna Singh are other highlights in the film.

INTERESTINGLY, THE three pivotal people involved in the making of the film, Akbar Khan, Kabir Bedi and Sonya Jehan visited the monument some months before the actual shooting began. Those waiting to visit this great mausoleum of love must take the next available flight to Agra. And those interested in knowing how it got built, how a great love story came to be, must make a beeline to the nearest air-conditioned theatre, and watch Akbar Khan's labour of love.

SURESH KOHLI

RIGHT FROM my childhood, I have fantasised about projects with huge canvasses, films by Cecil de Mille and David Lean, projects like *Lawrence of Arabia, Benhur, Elcid, Ten Commandments.* It has been fascinating watching these films, and identifying with some of the heroic characters as they appeared on the big screen. That coupled with the fact that I was a bad student in school except for history, which was my favourite subject even though I dropped out of school itself. So I always fantasised that whenever I get into filmmaking, I must make a historical and destiny did play a major role in my getting into making historicals when my brother Sanjay Khan met with a tragic accident during the making of *The Sword of Tipu Sultan.* I bore the responsibility of completing the project for him because everything got burnt during the first episode itself, in Mysore, and there were setbacks and tragedy.

AFTER THAT I got onto making *Akbar the Great,* which was probably the biggest television project of its time. So it was this passion for history that drove me towards historicals. But then the small screen was not what I was really aiming for. I wanted to one day translate my dream, my fantasy on the big colossal screen with stereophonic sound. And then I happened to visit the Taj Mahal. This was about ten years ago. I visited the Taj Mahal as a tourist. I saw a whole lot of foreigners with local guides looking spellbound at the magnificent structure. I was myself fascinated by its beauty.

I FELT hearts were pounding in the marble slabs, every rose petal, every leaf that was engraved in the multitude of colours was alive. And while listening to the tourist guides, telling the tremendous love story of Arjumand Bano, a young princess who falls in love with Prince Khurram, who finally becomes Shahjehan, the Emperor of Hindustan, I felt fascinated. How their love blossoms and becomes one of the greatest love stories, when the separation with Arjumand becomes a commitment for Shahjehan to create this monument in memory of not only his wife, but a monument in memory of a promise to his dying love moved me tremendously. And I decided to work on this love story.

THERE IS no doubt this is but the biggest film ever made in the Indian motion picture history. And one dare not attempt to make a film of this nature, this magnitude with a shoestring budget and a weak heart because then the commitment will be absolutely hollow. So once I decided to give shape to this dream of mine, no money aspect had to come in its way. No financier or distributor was going to dictate terms. And I told myself I would not start marketing it until its complete culmination. That is precisely what happened. Believe you me, no money and effort was spared to make the film the way I wanted to make it, and by the grace of God none of my collaborators, whether banks or individuals, ever questioned me on the making of the film. All my spending has been on the production values, and not on stars because my subject itself is the superstar, the content itself is the king. Besides, filmmaking is a human endeavour and despite best planning things do tend to sometimes go out of hand, and if some of the schedules went beyond stipulation, they had to, to get the right impact.

THE WHOLE film has been shot in 245 days over a period of two and a half years. Keeping in mind the scale on which it has been made, this can be called a record of sorts, considering the stipulations of the script. And without any compromise whatsoever! I had twenty-two sets constructed, each one of them elaborate enough to depict the golden era of the Moghul period — a *Diwan-e-khaas*, a *Diwan-e-awam*, *Rang Mahals*, *Tehekhanas*, prison cells, private chambers, an *Ibadat Khana*, a *Meena Bazaar*, *Sheesh Mahal*. Prince Khurram and Arjumand Bano had to sail in a boat, so I had one built to match the vessels of that period. For the action scenes we had to pitch hundreds of tents made in the ancient style and we nearly set up a small tent industry in our company. We even made a replica of Aurangzeb's grand tent. I exposed over 1000 cans of raw stock to get the battle sequences right.

A MAJOR highlight of the film is the construction of the Taj Mahal slab by slab. The audience gets to see the shell of the Taj Mahal, a half-built structure and then, the momument as it exists today. I have shown thousands of workers slogging away, animals carrying marble slabs, boats laden with materials landing on the banks of the river. These scenes are a combination of real shooting, special effects and computer graphics. I had my way. If I visualised a scene in a particular way, I shot it exactly that way. Most of the film was shot in Jodhpur where we leased the Mehrangarh Fort. That did not come cheap because we kept most of the 19 sets absolutely erect right through the making of the film, rather even during editing, should there have been some reshooting required. The film has also been shot extensively in Marwar, Jaipur, Udaipur, Nagor, and at the famed Nishat Bagh and Shalimar Garden in Kashmir. A part of one song was picturised along the Samurai river and other locales in Ladakh. All that required time and money, and I spared none.

I HAD envisaged a budget of Rs 50 crore when I started the film, and today all I can say is that I have not overspent, though I must also add that I stopped counting money during the making of the film, to achieve the desired effects. The first actor I signed was Kabir Bedi because I felt he was the only one who had the personality, the gait, the voice, and the presence that an emperor deserves. And my toughest job was to sign a young lad, a new man, and a new face that will be accepted as a dynamic prince, who would finally turn into an emperor that grows to be Kabir Bedi. I auditioned more than 200-300 young actors and models and none came close to my conception. Then one day my wife, Marium saw the photograph of a

model on the internet and that was Zulfikar, whom I have introduced as the young Shahjehan.

THEN CAME the issue of a girl, a face that would launch a thousand ships. I did consider Aishwarya Rai because of her beauty and talent. I even met her, but somehow I felt she wouldn't suit the requirements of the role considering she already had a strong image as an actress, and was also involved in many other projects and I did not want to run into date hassles once I started shooting. So after weighing all the pros and cons, I settled for a new face. I came across this girl Sonya Rizvi in London, and I knew instantly that I had found my Arjumand Bano Begum. So this is how it started, and as luck would have it, she had the pedigree. She is the granddaughter of the legendary singing star of yesteryears, Noorjehan, who moved to Pakistan after the Partition. I think she has done a wonderful job, and justified my faith in her abilities. She grew in confidence as the film progressed, and that's how I wanted it. The transformation from innocence to maturity, as in real life, was beautifully captured in her growth from Arjumand Bano Begum to Mumtaz Mahal.

SOON AFTER I started working on the script I had a chance meeting with Fatima Meer in South Africa. Her roots are in India. Her father was an Indian. She had seen *Akbar the Great* when it was telecast in South Africa. Her knowledge about India is amazing. So when I met her and requested her to co-write the script of *Taj Mahal*, she agreed. The film has been based on historical facts as available in numerous texts. Now we hadn't heard or read what transpired between different characters. So we had to extend our imagination and create words that different characters mouth in the film with historical data, the incidents, the places, the people and use this in a credible way to enhance the drama, to make it into a flowing narrative.

MY CHICAGO-based American associate felt it has great potential in North America. So it has been dubbed in English and is being released there besides me having prints for the Indian diaspora. The Americans prefer to hear the dialogue rather than read them. It has been subtitled in English for the European market. Besides English, I am dubbing it in Persian and Arabic. The fact that the image of the Taj Mahal is dominant in the minds of people travelling to India, as it inevitably appears in every brochure and other tourism promotional material should also help. So I feel it can reach all parts of the world.

I HAD no doubts regarding the music of the film, and did not have to go far to get it. It was fortunate that I had worked with Naushad saheb in both *The Sword of Tipu Sultan* and *Akbar the Great*, and I had known of his dedication. He has also been associated with the biggest Hindi film hits of historical nature. I felt he was the only one who could give credible music for a project of this kind. His enthusiasm betrays his age. It is the first film project he has undertaken in the last fourteen years. As a director, I had my own inputs. He was open to suggestions. So we clicked very well as a composer-director team, and the music is already enjoying a good report. I am sure it is the kind of music that would last. It will not be something that is released today and forgotten tomorrow.

AKBAR KHAN

Taj Mahal

Timur - I - Leng → Babur 1483 - 1530 r1526 - 1530

Hindal

Askari Ghiyas Beg

Kamran

Humayun
1508 - 1556 r1530 - 1556

Hakim

Asaf Khan

Mehrunissa (Noorjehan)

Arjumand (Mumtaz-i-Mahal)
1595-1630

Laadli

Sher Afkun

Shahriya

Kudsiya
1630 - 1706

Murad
1624 - 1661

Aurangzeb Alamgir
1618-1707 r1658 - 1707

Raushanara
1617 - 1671

Bahadur Shah
1643 - 1712 r1707 - 1712

Great Moghul Dynasty

Akbar 1542 - 1605 r1556 - 1605

- **Daniyal**
- **Murad**
- **Jahangir (Salim)** 1569 - 1627 r1605 - 1627

- **Shahjehan (Khurrum)** 1592 - 1666 r1627 - 1658
- **Parwez**
- **Khusrav**

- **Shahshuja** 1616 - 1660
- **Dara Shikho** 1615 - 1659
- **Jahanara (Begum Sahib)** 1614 - 1681

Reliving the Times

As they unfold...

1

Queen Noorjehan dotes on her daughter, Laadli Begum, begotten from her first husband. She, therefore, nurtures the dream of seeing her as the next queen. Both set their eyes on the brave and handsome Prince Khurram, who is not only his father's favourite, but also heir-apparent to the throne.

2

Although the film opens differently, at the centre are the enigmatic, powerful but justice-loving Emperor Jahangir, and his modern in outlook but manipulating and ambitious queen Noorjehan. When not attending to matters of statecraft, the emperor drowns himself in the finest of wines in the company of beautiful slave women in the palace's private chambers. The wise Noorjehan often chooses these moments to work on her husband to realise her ambitions.

3

When not engaged in either the affairs of the state, or beautiful slave dancing girls, the emperor likes to spend time with his favourite son, Prince Khurram, giving him not only tips in statecraft but also proudly extolling the extent and boundaries of the Moghul empire.

4

Moving away from the confines of the corridors of power, the young prince, unlike his other brothers, finds pleasure in outdoor adventure sport, often riding his favourite horse exploring parts of the beautiful kingdom he is set to inherit, and expand further. It is during one such adventurous outing that he comes across an innocent maiden, and he cannot take his eyes off her.

5

Arjumand Bano Begum, Queen Noorjehan's niece, lives in a dream world of her own. Naïve and unambitious, she remains aloof from palace politics and petty jealousies. She is blissfully ignorant of the vibrations she has unconsciously caused in Prince Khurram's heart.

6

Queen Noorjehan, who was greatly inspired by European lifestyles, often spent long hours in beauty treatment, getting her skin massaged in oils and herbs, luxuriating in tubs filled with cooling rose water. Here she is subtly warned about the young prince's interest in her niece.

7

The news of Prince Khurram's interest in Arjumand Bano flares tempers in Queen Noorjehan's quarters, and seems to shatter Laadli Begum's dreams of becoming the future queen and the love interest of the heir-apparent. He is of course ignorant of her aspirations towards him.

8

Queen Noorjehan begins to plot the fall of Prince Khurram. She prevails upon Mahawat Khan, her secret lover to create a situation, which will force the young prince to raise a cry of revolt, a defiant action that would bring him down in the esteem of his father. This would pave way for the elevation of another incompetent but ambitious son to the seat of power.

9

The scheme works to perfection. Prince Khurram rises in revolt not only to prove his innocence in any conspiracy against the emperor, but also to guard the honour of his ladylove, who too has become a target for the wily queen. Queen Noorjehan does not even mind sacrificing her brave brother in furthering her own interests and ambitions.

10

To ease brewing tension in the palace, and as a fall out deal with Noorjehan, Arjumand Bano decides to sacrifice her own love for Prince Khurram, and persuades him to marry Kandhari Begum who is Emperor Jahangir's choice as the bride for his favourite son, and heir-apparent.

11

Prince Khurram is arrested for the unpardonable crime of revolting against the emperor, and defying the royal orders. The defiant prince pleads not guilty, and vows to expose those behind the great conspiracy. He openly accuses Queen Noorjehan of her involvement in the great designs that led to his revolt.

12

Love does triumph in the end, and after a great deal of hue and cry and bargaining, the lovers ultimately unite, and even though Arjumand Bano Begum has to share her husband with some other beautiful wives about whom history is not very generous, she remains his first and most abiding interest.

13

In time, as their love prospers, Prince Khurram is duly proclaimed the Emperor Shahjehan, and Arjumand Bano Begum gets to be known as the benevolvent Queen Mumtaz Mahal. She bears him fourteen children. But it is during the last childbirth that she develops complications, and succumbs to them. She leaves behind a vacuum in the emperor's life, which he seeks to fill by working towards realising her last wish, the building of a mausoleum that would stand the test of time, and a living monument to their immortal love.

14

Emperor Shahjehan ages almost overnight. He starts to live a life of austerity, drapes himself in white robes, and embarks on a mission of realising Mumtaz's last wish. He takes an uncanny interest in the designing and architecture of the mausoleum, and supervises its construction during the next two decades, and more.

15

In keeping with the Moghul traditions laid down by Emperor Babar, Shahjehan declares his eldest son, Dara Shikho as the heir-apparent to the throne. The educated, liberal Dara is a thorn in the eyes of the hardcore Muslim fundamentalists, including his youngest brother, Aurangzeb, who considers him too soft, and totally incompetent to be the emperor. With the aid of his other brothers, whom he regards equally incompetent, Aurangzeb wages a war in which Dara is defeated, and taken prisoner, along with his son.

16

The cunning Aurangzeb gets his other brothers slain because he considered them incompetent, vulnerable. Having achieved that he orders the execution of Dara and his son.

17

On being informed about Dara Shikho's defeat, and fearing his safety, Shahjehan sends his favourite daughter Jahanara to Aurangzeb as an emissary. She comes with the royal sword as a symbol of Shahjehan's reluctant proclamation of his defiant young son as the new emperor.

18

Jahanara cries out in horror on receiving the slain head of her defeated eldest brother, Dara Shikho in the form of a dinner feast.

19

Aurangzeb is proclaimed the emperor after the formal coronation by the court.

20

After the formal coronation, Aurangzeb pays a courtesy visit to his father, Emperor Shahjehan, who is now being held captive in his royal chambers.

21

Jahanara is Shahjehan's only consolation now. She too is in captivity since Aurangzeb proclaimed himself the emperor. Shahjehan examines a pendant that daughter Jahanara started wearing after the demise of Mumtaz Mahal.

22

Dejected, sad and feeling thoroughly humiliated, Shahjehan shares his helplessness with daughter Jahanara, and requests her to visit Aurangzeb and seek permission to visit the grave of his beloved on the occasion of her death anniversary.

23

Jahanara visits her brother and Emperor Aurangzeb, who has already abandoned the regalia and is living like a commoner in austerity. He gives his elder sister a patient hearing, and grants his father permission to visit his mother's grave inside the Taj Mahal.

24

But it is all too late. By the time Jahanara arrives with the royal orders, Shahjehan's soul has already departed to seek a final reunion with his soulmate that has come to be known as the ultimate epitome of love, and separation.

The Performers

Arbaaz Ali as

Jahangir

Essaying a difficult role is the handsome young actor who seems to have got acting in his genes. Son of the late hero of yesteryears turned villian in later life, Ajit, Arbaaz Ali has also been a popular model who now has several plum assignments under his belt.

Arbaaz Ali

"I HAD been quite a fan of Akbar Khan ever since I saw his film, *Haadsa*, as a schoolboy. So I was delighted to get a call from his office. I think he had seen a picture of mine with one of his writers, Muhafiz Haider. So, when Akbar saheb told me that he wanted me to play a role, a certain role, I was more than delighted. But unfortunately, I had some problems and I could not essay that role. So sometime later, he summoned me again and narrated the role of Jahangir. The narration was simply mind-blowing. There were shades and possibilities in this character, which were simply not there in the other roles I had been taking on.

INITIALLY, AKBAR saheb had given me some tips. He asked me to go through some history books and get to know things about Jahangir. After that I was made to attend a workshop, where I practiced wearing those heavy costumes. During the making, I tried to improvise, tried to interpret the role as I understood it. And the director liked what I did. So one could say that our approach to the character was similar. But at the same time, I must confess that Akbar saheb is a very strong person, and if he wants something, he gets it. There were no shooting shifts as such, and we worked all the time, and not always in convenient circumstances, though I must confess no stone was left unturned to make us all feel comfortable. But one can well imagine how comfortable could one get shooting a costume drama in the dry heat of Jodhpur, and the make-up kept peeling off, and one did not necessarily feel fresh all the time.

Jahangir

THERE WAS nobody in the film I did not feel comfortable with. Zulfi is an old friend. Pooja and me have worked together before. Kim is a very easy person. Sonya was, of course, a newcomer, a very nice girl who made you feel comfortable whenever she was around. Arbaaz is again an old friend, we have grown up together. It was a delight watching Kabir saheb. He was an inspiration. So, I tried to work hard, and tried harder and harder because I realised that Akbar saheb is an actor himself. He was pushing us to the limits because he would be the first to arrive in the morning and pack up after everyone else had. And for an actor, who lived a very cushy life, to work that hard, actually, gave me the drive to work hard under the sun and I think that shows in my work. And I owe my performance, which I think is quite promising, to Akbar Khan.”

Pooja Batra as

Noorjehan

A former beauty queen, and a famous model, Pooja Batra quit acting for matrimony and a comfortable living with her doctor-husband in the United States, even before she had realised her full potential as an actress. Tall and statusque, she excelled in all the characters she portrayed on the Hindi screen. She lends poise and credence to the character of the majestic, though shrewd and ambitious, and colourful queen from the golden era of Indian history.

Pooja Batra as Noorjehan

"WHEN I was offered the role of Noorjehan, I was at that point in my career, where I had played mostly young, trendy women and was looking for something challenging and different. That's when I got a call from Akbar. I went to Jodhpur for a day to audition for the role of Jahanara and while I was there I asked him to let me read for the part of Noorjehan and left it to his discretion. A week later he called back asking me to play Noorjehan. It was a very exciting and challenging role for me. I had to do a lot of research on the character and the more I read about her the more intrigued I was. She was very intelligent, sophisticated, ambitious, authoritative and ahead of her time. And to project all this was not easy.

I READ multiple books including *The Feast of Roses*, *Power Behind the Veil*, Indu Sundaresan's *The Twentieth Wife* and Ellison Bank's *Noorjehan*, among others. Besides reading, Akbar's insight has been a great help in learning more about Moghul history in general. The way he explained the specific events made it so much easier to understand the emotions that Noorjehan must have gone through at that point of time. With his perspective, I tried to add nuances, which helped the character. But finally, after all is said and done, it is the actor's instinct that brings the character to the fore and that's what I trusted the most. There was a lot of subtext that had to be used to play her and this came from all the above. It was tough to fully portray such a magnificent lady and I hope I have achieved that. I have had an amazing time shooting for this film and the camaraderie amongst the actors and the crew was what kept us going in the cruel heat of the Rajasthan desert. I could not have chosen a better team of people to work with. Mr Rao, in particular, is a genius at his craft and makes the scenes come alive with his lighting and camera angles. Ultimately though, it has been Akbar's baby, he has put in the most work and created this project from ground zero. All the credit goes to him in putting this massive project together."

Introducing Zulfikar Syed as
Prince Khurram

A popular model and an upcoming actor, Zulfikar Syed's uncanny resemblance to Kabir Bedi, who had already been selected to play emperor Shahjehan, cast the vote in his favour. He was selected from amongst the couple of hundred others who had shown up for audition for the important role of Prince Khurram who goes on to become emperor Shahjehan.

Zulfikar Syed

"A LOT of my friends had gone and auditioned for the role of Prince Khurram. I knew about it but was reluctant until one fine morning I got a call from Akbar Khan's office. To my surprise, I was explained the character, and offered the role almost straightaway. That much seems simple but eventually a lot of effort had to be put in once the shooting went underway. I tried to interpret the character in my way, but it was Akbar saheb's conception and interpretation that, I guess, helped a great deal. A lot of work had to be done on the language. It was Urdu and even though my mother tongue is Urdu I did not understand many words. It was a great learning experience altogether.

I AM from Bangalore. I graduated from this city and in college people would say, that when I grow up I would look like Mr. Kabir Bedi. I would just laugh it all aside. And today, I am sort of playing young Kabir Bedi! My friends are shocked and surprised to say the least! I wasn't really apprehensive. He has played his role and I have played my role and I am confident about my job. It is now for the audience to decide. We never face one another in the film. It was a tremendous experience. I have learnt a lot from this movie. I was never afraid or apprehensive, and confident from the moment I entered the sets. I never really worried about the others in the shot. I would simply look into the camera and perform.

Prince Khurram

BUT HAVING said that, I must confess that I am a director's actor, and Akbar saheb has gone about making the movie with a great deal of patience, passion and dedication. He would always explain the background to the scene, and what kind of mood and emotion he expected. And that really helped. Everyone in the unit has worked very hard. My love interest in the film, Sonya, was also a great help. I don't think those intimate scenes would have come in as naturally had she not been equally involved in the role and the project. Those scenes were not easy to perform. And mind you, unlike me, she had been facing the camera for the first time. I think the fact that Akbar saheb understood the character thoroughly also helped me interpret and evolve it satisfactorily."

Introducing Sonya Jehan as

Mumtaz

An almost born intuitive actress, she had been pursuing a course in textile design at a famous London institute, when Akbar Khan accidentally met her at a friend's house and he knew straightaway that she was his Mumtaz Mahal. Grand daughter of the legendary singer-actress Noor Jehan who migrated to Pakistan after the Partition in 1947, Sonya Rizvi had art in her genes. A trained dancer, she fits into the role gracefully.

Sonya Jehan as Mumtaz

"WORKING IN the film was a great experience but I was overwhelmed. I felt very insecure; unsure of my capabilities as a newcomer, but at the same time I felt strong enough to go through it, because the crew and the unit had been very helpful. They were very supportive. There was a great blend of emotions. A lot of fighting, lots of laughter, lots of crying. But I am happy it has all been worth it and people are going to see the movie.

I MET Akbar in London and he told me that he wanted me to play this role. I was flattered but I wasn't too keen on playing Mumtaz. He was insistent though. He wanted me to fly down to Mumbai, and got upset on being told that I couldn't do that because I wanted to appear for my finals in printing and textiles. He called me again six months later, and this time I flew down to appear for a screen test. I was accepted for the role.

I HAD to do a lot of reading and also spend a lot of time with Akbar because he knows a lot about history. So just sitting with him and talking to him and the scriptwriter on the sets taught me who Mumtaz was. So that was my approach, rather casual, as Akbar also did not want me to know too much. He wanted me to have that look of insecurity on the screen. He wanted me to look a bit uneasy, a bit scared because that's how she is introduced in the film. And towards the end he wants to show her as a strong woman. Love has made her strong and she would do anything for her loved one."

Kabir Bedi as
Shahjehan

India's first truly international star, Kabir Bedi has tasted unprecedented success with Sandokan, *the Italian-German-French mini-series. He followed it up with a role in* The Bold and the Beautiful, *and the bad guy in the James Bond film,* Octopussy, *apart from several other international projects for stage, television and cinema. Back home Kabir Bedi has starred in more than 50 films in a career spanning more than three decades, beginning with Girish Karnad's* Tughlaq. *The Shakespearean tragedy,* Othello *is his most memorable play. He has also starred in the London production of* The Far Pavilion.

Kabir Bedi

"IT IS the kind of role I had always hoped I would play one day. And when Akbar offered me the role of the older Shahjehan, I just leapt at the opportunity. It was a challenge not just in terms of falling back on all that I had learnt in theatre and in international film, but also being able to get under the skin of the elegant Urdu language, as opposed to merely memorising dialogue. In terms of preparation, being a student of history, I knew a fair amount about Shahjehan anyway. But I actually went back to the Taj Mahal two months before we started shooting, just to see it and get a sense of the man from what he had created. It was quite an awesome experience. Just the size of the monument is awesome, apart from anything else. So, it has been a journey of discovery for me, as much of my own capabilities as that of the most important figures in Indian history.

INITIALLY, I had to try and enter the mind and spirit of this emperor, who apart from having lived one of the greatest love stories of the world, built the greatest symbol of love that the world has ever known. He was also one of the greatest builders. And what is interesting about the structure of the film, and the way Akbar has conceptualised it, is that it begins with Shahjehan in his final crisis, where his own son is usurping him of his throne and the whole love story is a series of flashbacks.

Emperor Shahjehan

BEYOND MY own work on the role, I really have to salute and thank Akbar for being such an enormous support and inspiration. A thousand *salaams* for giving me the role and also the freedom to interpret it in ways that suited me. Initially, when we started, there was some friction because there were differences of style and how I imagined certain scenes should be shot. And Akbar was very clear, yet very flexible. He was so certain about the results he wanted and yet flexible enough to know how he got there. So, whatever minor teething troubles we had were ironed out very quickly.

ABOVE ALL, I have to salute Akbar's extraordinary courage in mounting a film of this scale, this expense and this vision without casting Bollywood's top box-office stars. Akbar has, in a sense, even risen above himself in the process by assembling a team of great talent. So something very special has come out and Akbar has brought all of us together.”

Manisha Koirala as

Jahanara

One of the most glamourous and accomplished actresses of the Hindi screen ever since she made a debut in Saudagar, *Manisha Koirala has acted in nearly a hundred films in the past decade and a half, working opposite almost all the top heroes from Amitabh Bachchan to Shah Rukh Khan. Born and brought up in Nepal, Manisha has now made Mumbai and India her second home, and continues to be in demand for roles demanding intesity.*

Manisha Koirala as Jahanara

"I WAS reluctant when Akbar asked me if I would be interested, since he was taking someone new for the main role. But I agreed when he showed me the research work and I felt I should do it, because he is going to be doing something new, something different. His sincerity impressed me and I decided to be a part of it. It was a flattering experience. I have thoroughly enjoyed getting ready for the whole thing. I just love the costumes and the jewellery! I enjoyed shooting with Akbar because he is extremely sincere about his work, and I love that sincerity in people, otherwise you feel you are wasting your time, you are working with people who are not interested in their work, their mind is not focused, and that is the kind of thing I like to stay away from. I found Akbar not only extremely focused, but at work also he was very relaxed and full of fun, both while shooting and after pack-up.

AKBAR EXPLAINED the subtleties of the role to me, he made me understand the relation between the father and the daughter, which was enough for me, something to which I related very well, because I am very close to my father. So the emotional protectiveness that Jahanara felt for her father came naturally to me. It wasn't difficult for me to understand the character, the emotions behind it, and the reason behind her being the kind of person she was. Akbar's interpretation, and explanations were also very helpful. His grasp on the script, and the various characters was amazing, and so also his commitment to the project. I have rarely seen that sort of devotion in the Indian film industry. I have not worked in a unit which despite its enormity, appeared so cohesive and disciplined. It is all a tribute to Akbar Khan."

Arbaaz Khan as
Aurangzeb

Younger brother of one of the current heart throbs, Salman Khan, and son of scriptwriter Salim Khan (of the famous erstwhile Salim-Javed duo), Arbaaz Khan has been born with cinema in his blood. He has carved out a niche for himself through a variety of negative roles he has convincingly essayed in nearly a dozen films since his debut some years ago. He has risen to the demands of the script and justified the maker's faith in his capabilities.

Arbaaz Khan

"IT WAS a great experience working in Akbar Khan's film for the simple reason that there are very few filmmakers who do extensive work and have so much love and passion for their product that economics don't dictate the quality of film being made. He had done an amazing amount of study on the film prior to starting the movie. I did a little bit of homework. There is very little in terms of references that one can examine. When you approach a historical character, like Aurangzeb, all that there is to be known is to look at sketches and whatever is there in history books.

MY INPUT was how to use my personality in the best possible way to project that particular character, because finally you are the instrument — your body, or your voice, or your personality is going to project a character that was in history, and that no one has really seen. So I tried to read as much as I could about the character. But the major help came from my director himself, with his meticulous research on that entire era and that period in particular, and more so, for me, on this very character.

I SPENT a lot of time with Akbar Khan in trying to know as much as he knew about Aurangzeb, and trying to gauge from what he spoke about the personality — his temperament, the level of his integrity, his honesty, his anger, his ego. And once you know this, you tend to form an image of the particular person and try to project it to the best of your ability.

Aurangzeb

I ALSO read some interesting books I could lay my hands on, like *The Peacock Throne*, and *The Great Moghuls*. So I got a little familiar with the atmosphere of that period, and I did as much as I could, getting close to the impression of, or the effect of what Aurangzeb was. I am sure to some extent my looks and family background must have helped Akbar Khan decide in my favour to essay this demanding role.

I HAVE played a lot of negative characters in my short span as an actor. In all those films, the characters I portray are not only contemporary, urban individuals who are either born villians or those who become so because of the circumstances. But in *Taj Mahal*, I try to relive a character who is totally honest, and convinced about his righteousness. I hope my interpretation and depiction of Aurangzeb shows this much maligned character from Indian history in his true, natural perspective."

Laadli Begum

KIM SHARMA, who made her debut in the blockbuster, *Mohabbatein* some years ago, and is struggling to establish herself as a competent actress, essays the role of empress Noorjehan's first daughter, Laadli Begum, who has her eyes set on the throne of Hindustan.

Dara Shikho

VAQUAR SHEIKH essays the role of Dara Shikho, the eldest son of Shahjehan and Mumtaz Mahal and heir to the throne. He was greatly interested in carrying forward the legacy of his great grand-father, Akbar who sought to assimilate the diverse faiths into one religion.

Kandhari Begum

An international ramp model and actress from Norway who has acted in Hindi cinema, Negar Khan tries to bring to life the forgotten first wife of Prince Khurram from Persia, who unfortunately, does not live long to have a decisive role in history.

Mahawat Khan

MILIND GUNAJI, a very accomplished stage and screen actor, essays the role of Mahawat Khan, one of the great army Generals in Jahangir's army who is besotted with empress Noorjehan and is manipulated by her to achieve her ends.

Behind the Scenes

Anna Singh

She is an astounding success story in the highly competitive world of mainstream Hindi cinema. Barely 35, this Gold Medalist from JJ School of Arts, Mumbai in Textile Culture, Design Content and Commercial Art, has not only designed costumes for alomost all the leading artistes of the film industry in over 550 films, she also has the distinction of doing the personal wardrobe for Michael Jackson when he first visited India for a concert.

Regalia

I HAD known Akbar for many years, had even designed costumes for him at some point. I ran into him one day at the Mumbai airport. He was off to Jodhpur, and some other places. He mentioned this project and we decided to meet in his office a week later. The meeting was very inspiring, considering that you do not have movies of this magnitude being made every second day. So obviously, it was very exciting and whatever I saw in his office; the detailed paper work, models, work-plans, the amount of effort, the intricacies being sorted out all that enticed me to join in, and that was it. It was one and a half years of intense working on the movie, plus the research for three months. When we researched, we researched every single person, what kind of ego, eccentricities the people had, the kind of mental hang-ups; we tried to incorporate all these nuances in the style of working, and all of it was done on location.

IT WAS fun and hard work. We did a lot of improvisation. Akbar gave me total freedom. He was always open to suggestions, ready to sort problems that one was having on the sets. He has that intrinsic ability to deal with it, and make it easier for you. He did not want to compromise on anything. Since he seemed to have given some sort of history lessons to all his artistes, it made things easier. I had my little office on location. It was an unforgettable experience. I don't think I have worked harder, and enjoyed every bit of it in any other project. And mind you, I have worked on the costumes of maybe a million stars. Thank you, Akbar. You were a wonderful person to work with.

USING MINIATURE paintings and other available visual material of the Moghul period as the basis, and taking into account the requirements of various historical characters, Anna Singh designed costumes, headgear and jewellery. She shifted her headquarters to the Jodhpur location for one and a half years, undertook extensive research not only by studying the script but any relevant details available through even secondary texts, pondering over the characters, their specific moods in the context of the scenes, keeping an eye on the architecture and designs of the respective sets in terms of colours and patterns used before using fabric, weaves, cuts and jewellery.

THIS WAS generally more metaphoric with some colours representing passion, wealth, power, position, and some a total lack of it, but never compromising on the aesthetics. The same applies to the use of jewellery, especially worn by the women. In this monumental task, she received the unstinted support of her cutters, tailors, and artisans. For the fabric, she relied heavily on *jamawar* silks. Special pearls from China, and semi-precious stones were deployed and set to perfection in the ornamentation of costumes, jewellery, royal swords, daggers and headgears.

APART FROM designing costumes for the principal characters in the cast, a whole army of people had to be dressed. Having based it entirely on visual and written references available in primary and secondary texts, costumes had to be designed with

fabric, the cut and tailoring matching the position and status of the character. Costumes were made for the entire staff in the palace arena occupied both by the emperor and the empress and their immediate attendants, the princes and the princesses and their personal staff, the concubines, the royal guards; the gear and armour for the animals — the saddles and embellishments for the horses, the *hoodahs* and coverlets for the elephants complete with other embellishments — Totems, flags, bells.

AT THE end, it was impossible to keep an account of the textile rolls used; the length of threads, and their colours; and zari deployed to enrich the costumes worn. The footwear proved no exception. Any production house would be hard pressed to find display space for the material, and it is anyone's guess, if a proper account could have been kept for every single element used, what it would come up to.

A TOTAL of 19,418 buttons and hooks were used. About 160 kg of small mirrors. About 1600 dresses had to be stitched complete with footwear, armbands, and shields for those deployed in the war sequences. A total number of 16,119 junior artistes were employed during the shooting of various scenes, while 8,761 craftsmen worked round the clock to prepare the costumes and the sets. Each costume of the principal female character had 15 pieces — *dupatta* (the veil), face-wrap linen, earrings, bangles, nose and finger rings, bracelets, *tikka* (forhead jewellery), hair adornments, armband, waistband, choker, necklace, *paizebs* (anklets), and the shoes.

THE SAME, though not to the same extent, was the case with men. Here the key areas were the pearl necklaces, and semi-precious gems were used in the headgears and crowns. The number of wigs, especially used by Emperor Shahjehan, both in his youth and the adult years. The variation of costumes in the case of this pivotal character alone required special care, as the character underwent personality changes, from a king in royal regalia to a recluse in pastels and whites.

THE MAKE-UP material is yet another reference point when dealing with the work that went into working on the faces of the artistes in the exasperating desert heat.

"Eventually, when everything came together, when the cast put on their attires, their jewellery and headgear, just seeing them walk into the various scenes was something to feel content about, a certain feeling of satisfaction and pride entered my being, because I had designed it all, something that was my creative contribution and could not have been bought off the shelf anywhere."

"When Shahjehan,
the king of angelic properties,
Arose from the throne of life
and set out for the hereafter,
I sought from reason the year of this event,
And Wisdom told me;
"The King of the World has died".

Anonymous

C.B. More

Chandrakant More had assisted some of the more established art directors, worked in more than a 100 films as an assistant art director, including Vijaypath, Border, Kurukshetra *and a 3-D extravaganza,* Abracadabra *before he, like many others, got an independent break with this film.*

WHEN AKBAR Khan saheb invited us for a discussion in his office we had no idea what he had in mind for us. And our excitement knew no bounds when he offered us the art direction of the film. We pondered over the offer for some time before accepting the assignment but at that time I did not realize that ultimately the whole thing will fall on my shoulders alone as my senior and associate fell sick.

WE HAD lots of discussions. Akbar Khan saheb briefed us about his conception of various sets, showed us a lot of books and sketches. We visited almost all the historical places, forts etc. to assess the ambience and get a feel. I visited several libraries and consulted books relating to that time, took my own notes and drew up sketches. But while I did all that I still did not have a proper assessment of the magnitude as I had not got a sense of the director's vision. That turned out to be challenging as well as a blessing-in-guise. It gave me an opportunity to prove not only to the rest of the film industry but even to myself what I was capable of doing.

WE TRAVELLED through half the length of the country before we settled on the fifteenth century Mehrangarh fort in Jodhpur. The ambience of a real fort helped us in putting up sets that looked realistic. But then this also added to the task, how and where to get capable work force to create sets of the magnitude required. Since the logistics of importing the labour from Mumbai were unrealistic we had to train local masons, carpenters, painters to create 19 sets in a span of more than a year at the same place.

ALL SAID and done, decorating those huge sets was not as easy as putting up the structures. So we used miniature paintings as reference material to design the arches, the gangways, thrones, props and other artifacts. We borrowed some authentic props from actual owners. Akbar saheb is a visionary and a very hard task master. He was never satisfied with merely looking at the drawings and sketches, so we had to make miniature sets. The most difficult was the replication of Taj Mahal itself. After a lot of deliberation and discussion we used white instead of yellow marble keeping in mind the fact that we were trying to recreate the time when the monument had just been built.

WHILE WE can take credit for all the hard work, it wouldn't have been possible without Akbar saheb's patience, and generosity. No amount of time, effort and money was spared to make every frame of the film look real. I will forever remain grateful to him for having faith in my abilities and giving me an opportunity to do this ambitious film.

Many of the artifacts, weapons and other materials on the sets have been made exactly as they would have been about 400 years ago!

THE COMPLETE film was first planned on paper, with almost nothing left to speculation except, perhaps, a last minute creative input. Every set was meticulously planned. Apart from the visual texts and reading materials made available by the producer, CB More visited libraries and reading rooms to explore other possibilities related to Moghul art and architecture. Having done all the paper work, and worked on the nuts, bolts and designs, the problem was to find a centralised location which would provide enough space to construct the interiors and exteriors of huge palace structures. The producer-director and the assistant art director, promoted to full stature, toured the entire country before zeroing down on the fifteenth century Mehrangarh Fort in Jodhpur. Eventually, the ambience of a real fort, as against an open piece of land, which had historical relevance — even though not directly related to the subject-period — lent authenticity and background to the real life drama being re-enacted for the silver screen.

MEHRANGARH FORT ultimately became the playground for the re-enactment of tension, intrigue, emotion, romance, happiness and joys, traumas and tragedies that were to set into motion the gradual decline of the glorious Moghul era in India. The nineteen huge sets consisting of the royal residential chambers, the public and the special halls of administration, the *Sheesh Mahal*, or the Glass Palace, the *Meena Bazaar*, or the modern-day gold souk, the prison cells, the lush green gardens blooming with a million flowers of different hues and colours were replicas of history, and the characters who inhabited them. The *Meena Bazaar* set was so monumental that it took the cinematographer three full days to light it up for the long ambience shot. Each little nook and corner was detailed from all that history books could offer in terms of text and visual material.

MINIATURE PAINTINGS of the Moghul period were used as reference material to design the thrones, the arches, the gangways and corridors, the ceiling and floor décor, the beds and bedchambers, the linen, the chairs and the lounges, the lighting system and other artifacts that look casually displayed in various parts of a specific scene of action. Also difficult to design, decorate and light were the royal ladies' quarters keeping their individual dress tastes in mind and synchronising the costumes and the background colours. Equally challenging was the construction of pleasure chambers, or the big recreation halls, which could accommodate the royalty and senior ministers.

EMPRESS NOORJEHAN'S chambers were to have colours and décor that reflected her European taste. Even her bathroom had to depict the influence. Old Emperor Shahjehan's living chambers after he was held a prisoner had to reflect his sombre moods, in keeping with the whites and pastels he had started to wear, and mostly devoid of rich colours, gems and stones that he had been so enamoured with in his youth. It had to be in complete

Facing page ***This is the replica of the dressing table of Mumtaz Mahal, painstakingly recreated with some pictorial and written references. The minute hand engraving on this table alone took two weeks and five crafts-men to complete.***

This set is the recreation area of the Laal Mahal or the room that was used during childbirth. Mumtaz bore her fourteenth child and breathed her last in these chambers. This set was built at the Mehrangarh Fort and was the room of the famous 'Zubeida' who married into the Rajput clan.

contrast to the richness visible in his living, first as Prince Khurram, and then as Emperor Shahjehan. Princess Arjumand Bano Begum's chambers, before she was renamed Mumtaz Mahal after Shahjehan's ascendancy to the throne, had to wear a simple, spartan look in keeping with her low profile status in the royal hierarchy. Colours and textures had to be borne in mind. Every royal chamber had to have exquisitely embroidered *chiks* or reed wall mats. So, instead of exercising the option of embroidering all the *chiks,* designs themselves were painted on them. The delectable eye-appeasing *kaleens* or carpets were both painted and hand woven. The mats, footrests, side tables, fruit trays and various other decorative artifacts were crafted to replicate the originals that existed almost 400 years ago.

EVERY LITTLE detail pertaining to the sets and décor had to go through the bounce-board effect between the chief architects and planners involved in the making of the magnum opus. Long discussions were held, with references being pulled up and sets drafted and miniatures created before the finals approved. It was a creative hegemony of the real and the imagined that went into the making of the sets and the film eventually. A method had to be devised even in replication. The decision to use white marble instead of the cream or pale yellow which is how the great monument seemingly appears today — was one such hallmark decision because the film depicts the period, when the *Taj Mahal* had just been commissioned, and using slightly coloured stone would have been self-defeating in the first place itself.

IN ORDER to lend further authenticity to the various edifices, structures and décor, the art director resorted to borrowing authentic pieces from actual descendants or inheritors. The lights had to produce candle light effect. *Mashaals* or torches and other traditional forms of lighting were set to use, but fire safety norms had to be borne in mind. The number of candles deployed during the entire indoor shoot made the art director lament in exasperation, "We feel we must have used more candles in this film than what must have been used in the entire seventeenth century."

SINCE IT was neither feasible nor practical to import experienced craftsmen, artisans and workers from Mumbai — both in terms of sheer volume and economics, local talent was hired, trained and deployed for assistance. Apart from more than a hundred masons, carpenters, painters, engravers, another couple of hundred were put into service to ready the sets for lighting and shooting. More than 9,000 sheets of hardboard and plywood were used in creating convincing replicas of the original grandeur. Nearly 480 artisans worked for more than 18 months to create these replications.

A challenging job always brings out the best in an artist. When Akbar Khan assigned C.B. More the art direction of his magnum opus 'Taj Mahal - An Eternal Love Story', instinctively C.B. More knew that he would reach the pinnacle of his career with this project.

Top Picture

Meena Bazaar - where Prince Khurram and Princess Arjumand Bano set eyes on one another

The opulent set of Sheesh Mahal, or the Glass Palace, which also served as the royal pleasure chambers.

C.B. More has also used some authentic pieces in the film. These have been on loan from the owners who were as excited as the makers were about the project. Keeping in mind that the lighting would have to be similar to candle light, mashaals or torches and other traditional forms of lighting were used. As a result one of the earliest concerns were on fire safety and insurance of the authentic pieces. Lighting, specifically candlelight, became a collaboration between the art department and the camera and light crew.

SOME OF the props required exceptional care and detail. Small things like spittoons, hand bowls, hand fans, games, partitions, stamps, engraved letters, quill pens, make up essentials etc., were fine-tuned to the minutest details.

Sham Kaushal is an action director par excellence. With films like Prahaar, Fiza, Hum Dil De Chuke Sanam, Asoka, Devdas, Pinjar *and* Lakshya *under his belt, his action credibility is befitting that of the moghul dynasty! The war sequences with over two hundred horses, about a hundred elephants and managing a warring crowd of a thousand odd people, keeping in mind the limitations of the historic era, is an achievement in itself.*

Arms and the Men

Sham Kaushal

"IT WAS a big challenge to work on a big film and it was something we were looking forward to. We planned a lot. We had so many meetings. Everything was planned on paper before we went to the location to shoot the war sequences with 400-500 horses and elephants. A whole lot of local, untrained people had to be used, their movements had to be monitored, their safety ensured. We would be there on location days in advance — sit there, plan things, visualize things, essentially because there is no scope for retakes when you are executing war sequences with huge crowds. Then, while we could trust the trained members with real weapons, we could not take chances with the locals, who were provided with look-real kind of armoury. We used fibre and rubber costumes, headgears, etc., so that people should not get hurt. It involved massive planning and by God's grace everything went smoothly. The result surpassed our expectations and the final product is par excellence. I kept praying during those shoots that no one should get hurt! Since I had earlier done *Asoka*, the experience helped.

IT WAS a wonderful experience working with a director like Akbar Khan. We worked more like comrades, brothers. There was complete bonding. The director had a distinctly clear vision. He did not want to compromise, and that helped. He was involved in the planning and execution of the shots on a day-to-day basis. We had no problems, no differences during the making, which is so rare in India. I think the action sequences in this film are my best work till date. We worked like a team, and a marvellous experience led to a marvellous result."

Arms and the Men

THE BIGGEST problem, according to action director Sham Kaushal, was to find places where action and war sequences could be freely shot, with the least risk to the trained and untrained junior artistes, and principal actors. The location also required none or minimal modern structures in the background. Once the locations were finalised, the problem of finding horses was an issue because it was physically impossible to transport 500 horses from one location to the other. Then came the task of training non-professionals because there were hardly 150 stunt artists registered with the association in Mumbai. So locals had to be deployed.

NOW MOTIVATING locals and getting work out of them was a Herculean task, especially making them understand the nitty-gritties; making the riders understand the finer nuances of battle sequences, and the discipline. The execution of the war sequences with all that dust which makes visibility minimal — but an essential prerequisite in such scenes — was a challenge. Bombs had to be planted. The trained guys could see those spots, but not the locals, more so the ones running behind the riders who could miss those marks in the frantic movement. "We planned lots," says the action director. "Before we went for the day's shoot, we worked all our movements on paper, including camera placements. We had to ensure minimal reshoots. It was massive planning and by the grace of God everything went very smoothly. Not a single casualty."

THE FAMOUS battle of Samugarh, which was a clash of more than 2,000 soldiers, had been fought just eight kilometre east of Agra, causing civil war during the reign of Shahjehan. A crew of about 3,000 re-enacted this sequence alone in the scorching heat of Jaipur. A total of 16,119 junior artistes were deployed in capturing the various war sequences. The costume department made about 1,600 uniforms, complete with headgear, footwear, armbands, leg pads and other accessories. Coverlets, saddles, accessories were also stitched for 500 elephants and 2000 horses. Over 40,000 yards of material was used only in drapes and covers.

RECASTING OF weapons and accompaniments was a no less daunting and ambitious project. History is replete with references about the grandeur of the Moghul period but very minimal visual material is available. A lot of time-consuming research and crosscheck of references had to be put in motion in order to cast and mould the armaments in fibreglass or rubber. Headgear, in particular. Since a lot of amateur and local talent had to be deployed in the war sequences, they could not be relied upon to handle actual and heavy arms and armour. So look-alikes were recreated and used. This was also necessary because the original armour weighed around 36 kilograms.

The swords and shields weighed about 15 kilogram, apiece. All the war attire had to be replicated in lightweight material, porous enough for ventilation. Shooting in the no-man's land in desert outdoors, with full make-up, and complete attire was hell re-lived, not only for the principal actors but also the vast secondary numbers of cast and crew for days on end.

A LOT of weapons were actually recast. Jewel-embellished *khanjars* (knives), spears and swords for the use of the royals were all custom made. Many of the props demanded skillful handling.

Little props, like spittoons, hand bowls, games, stamps, hand fans, engraved letters, quill pens, make-up essentials, partitions, tables and stools were crafted with minutest detail and extraordinary expertise.

Brothers at war:
Aurangzeb and Dara Shikho

He is, perhaps, the longest living and most honoured film music director in the country. He has composed music for nearly 70 films in a career spanning more than six decades, including Mother India, Ganga Jamuna, Pakeezah *to name just a few. Naushad Ali is the Chairman of Indian Performing Rights Society.*

Musical Compositions

Naushad Ali

"I HAD worked with Akbar Khan before when he was making his serial, *Akbar the Great*, some years ago. So when he came to me for *Taj Mahal*, narrated the subject to me I was moved by his passion. I almost instantly agreed to provide music for the film because historicals are nothing new to me. But I have tried to do something different, yet rooted in the Indian classical traditions. The picturisation of the songs has been excellent. The qawwali that he has picturised on the fabulous set of a *sheesh mahal* is out of the world. So also the picturisation of the raga, which would have been difficult for any director. He has done it all very aesthetically. I salute Akbar Khan's courage in doing such a picture in these times. It requires sheer madness to go in for such a subject, and such music. But then the audiences have always taken what it has been served. We are responsible for their tastes.

HAVING SAID that, I must confess it wasn't altogether easy composing music for this film. There were times when I did not like his interventions, while I was composing a certain tune. I am not used to that. But on later thoughts, I tried to incorporate those suggestions. One had to keep the audiences in mind. I think Naqsh Lyallpuri has done a great job with the theme song, which has been picturised very thoughtfully, and sung soulfully by Hariharan, who I thought was the only singer today with that kind of range, and breath."

Son of the renowned novelist Adil Rashid, Syed Gulrez has been exposed to literature and poetry right from childhood. Writing was a hobby that bloomed into a profession when he penned soulful ghazals for the award winning film Kamla *and nostalgic poems for none other than the great sufi singer Nusrat Fateh Ali Khan in* Salaam. *He is presently working on a few scripts in America.*

The Spoken Word Syyed Gulrez

"TO BEGIN with, I would sure love to say that working with Akbar Khan was a nostalgic memory come alive. As we had been together for his previous film, *Haadsa*, the mega epic, *Taj Mahal*, was in a way more than just a pleasant surprise. It all began in his office, and the meeting that would otherwise end with a cup of coffee soon turned into an association that eventually lasted more than two years. These memorable years not only saw me transforming his dream on paper as dialogue but added lengths to my admiration for him. Akbar Khan has not only matured with time but has acquired a unique touch in his approach towards film making. He is not only a perfectionist himself, but also demands perfection from all those he works with. And so be it, I thought and that was it.

I WAS initially signed for dialogue, but then as a hawk for talent that he is, I ended up penning the lyrics for this mega project. *Taj Mahal* is not just a film, it's a dream come alive. It's an endeavour that deals not only with romance, not just confined to mere history, but also has dealt with an entire era of the Moghul dynasty. *Taj Mahal*, the film has been completed but the memories of the maker Akbar Khan would dwell in my memory for decades to come.

IT SURE was an honour to be writing for Akbar Khan. It has been a privilege to dress his dreams in dialogue and his romantic feels in songs to remember. All I can say is that, if my dialogue are powerful and my songs a heart throb, the soul behind it all is none else then the mega maker of the great epic."

In a career spanning four decades, R.M. Rao has helped shape the history of India's advertising and documentary films through the lens of his motion picture camera. A graduate from the FTII, he has worked with major film makers and has demonstrated his flair for innovation and mastery over technique in a simple manner, in a career spreading over four thousand advertising films, about two hundred documentaries and seven feature films.

Having reached the pinnacle of success, Rao continues to shoot around the world showing remarkable energy and enthusiasm for the medium, which he confesses, is his first love.

The Moving Image

R. M. Rao

"I HAVE worked with many experienced directors but working with Akbar Khan was an entirely new experience. Having done historicals for television made him the ideal director to handle a historical film of this nature. As the cinematographer, I was fortunate to get enough time to plan an array of camera moves and have a cohesive lighting plan for every situation. My main concern, when we first began work on the project, was to visually interpret the sources of light true to the style of the times. In keeping with the period, interior lighting had to suggest candlelight and fire light. Keeping in mind the cinematic details of massive historic interiors, I tried to blend this look with traditional glamour lighting of the characters, pleasing song and dance situations and the varying moods of dramatic situations.

LOOKING BACK on the project, I am glad at the manner it has shaped up. However, the nature of cinematography is such that with every successive viewing one finds little details that one might want to alter. I look at this positively, and it lets me see the same situations in a new 'light' every time. I think the film has turned out well, and I am confident that it will stand out as an important landmark in Indian historical films in terms of performances, music, direction and, undoubtedly, in cinematography.

I THINK Akbar Khan's perseverance is remarkable, but being a perfectionist himself, who had mentally set out certain standards and the effects he had visualised, he sat through patiently as the light boys sweated out to create the proper lighting for the huge sets that had been constructed to recreate a bygone era. He always kept a vigil on what was happening, while simultaneously being involved in detailing costumes, jewellery and sets to perfection, and discussing the scenes with the artistes."

Widely hailed as one of the most innovative choreographers in the Hindi film industry, Saroj Khan has carved out a special niche for herself ever since she branched out on her own nearly three decades ago. She has not only the distinction of making almost all the leading heroes and heroines, especially the current crop, emulate her steps but at times even contributed to at least the musical success of the films. Saroj Khan has worked for nearly countless films, and shows no signs of tiring.

Choreography Saroj Khan

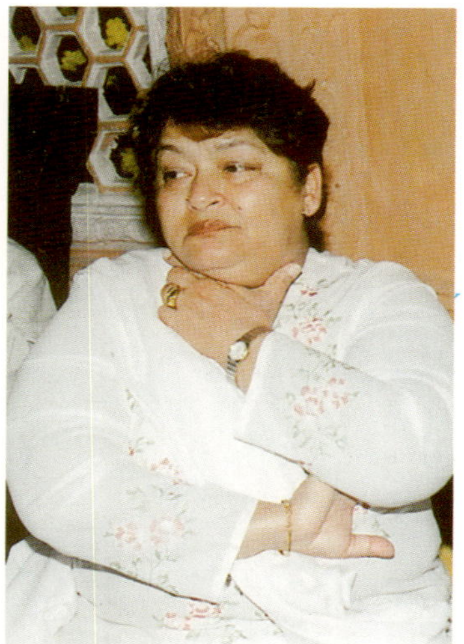

"ONE DAY I got a call from Akbar Khan to say that he was making *Taj Mahal*. I was very happy to hear that because I had worked in the earlier *Taj Mahal* (in the early sixties) with my guru, B. Sohanlal, and now I was getting a chance to independently work in a similar project. So I was very thrilled. I was also thrilled because I had even wanted to work with Akbar Khan when he was making *Haadsa* but had lost out to someone else. All the songs in the film are very expressive unlike the lyrics in today's films that hardly seem to contain any romance, and whatever little there is gets lost out because those enacting are somewhat impersonal. Today nobody is bothered about facial expressions, or feelings or emotions. Choreography is hardly used to heighten romance

BUT THE lyrics and music of this film are able to transport us back to that era when romance looked sensuous, and there was enough scope for the choreographer to be creative and innovative without seeming gimmicky. I have enjoyed doing this film. Besides, Akbar Khan has been very supportive, listening to my suggestions, and providing his own inputs without being interfering. Many of Akbar Khan's ideas are beautiful because he is a romantic and has been likened to a watchman of a bygone era when romance was divine and music an instrument to heighten the effect. He couldn't have got a better person than Naushad saheb to musically recreate that era.

SO I would say Akbar and me have been two ancient souls who have got together to do something...something that will be memorable."

Starting as an assistant in 1980, Sanjay Verma got an independent break with Khoon Bhari Maang, *and hasn't looked back since then. This film won him the coveted* Filmfare Award *for best editing. He has since repeated this performance thrice, apart from some other prestigious awards.*

The Cutting Edge

Sanjay Verma

"THIS IS is my first historical film as an editor. One had to be extra careful. It took us a lot more than normal time because there were these sequences, big sequences, numerous dramatic scenes, war shots, which we had to discuss many times over. So we would do it once, re-do it again and took every precaution that a historical film needed. We had to work out a totally different editing pattern. Normally one goes cut by cut, and the editing is very fast but this being a period film, we had to give it all the time. And hats-off to the director. I think he has done a marvellous job. He seemed to have mentally edited the sequences before executing them. The war shots are simply stunning. The film shaped up very well, indeed. The casting is superb. The hero has real good looks. The heroine is gorgeous, and looks regal. She is very pretty. Even the other casting is as mind-blowing, especially Pooja Batra, who has done a marvellous job.

ON THE whole, I think the film has been shot to perfection. All the ingredients and all the good vibes, which a historical film should have, are incorporated. I think producer Akbar Khan deserves full marks in assigning the direction to Akbar Khan!"

Optical Illusions

Venkat Krishnan

A self-taught artist who began his career as a painter and graphic designer simultaneously, Chennai-based technical expert, A Venkatakrishnan gradually moved to Aesthetics and Applied Art before turning a full-time computer graphic artist using Eyeon's digital fusion, softimage XSI and Maya. After doing special effects for ace-director Sangeetam Srinivas Rao's Tamil feature in 1995, he set himself as a full-fledged VFX supervisor and consultant for nearly half-a-dozen Tamil and Telegu feature films, apart from working on numerous short films and ad campaigns in South India. Taj Mahal *is his first major Hindi assignment.*

"AFTER THE initial brief from the director, I was really fascinated with the entire project as I saw the potential challenge awaiting me. It felt larger than life because we were to provide every VFX solution. It was time to get down to work and rebuild the Taj. We researched the architecture, building materials, methods and the design intricacies.

IT WAS not easy to be satisfied with our own work, because we had seen the real creation and we were creating not a 350-year-old Taj, but a brand new Taj as it would have looked on completion. Then, we moved on to modelling the structure. We had our equivalent of the architects, engineers, artisans and hard workers in our team, with our trusted tools...Maya, Softimage XSI, Digital Fusion, Photoshop and other inter-format aids. We worked with multiple hands and single- minded for 13 months and finally we did rebuild the Taj.

APART FROM constructing the Taj, there was yet another creation in the hands of our team...Oh yes! Deer...live deer. At first, like everyone else, we went ahead to shoot live deer with an idea to composite at the end. Well, it didn't work this time due to various reasons. And the confidence of having rebuilt the very Taj flashed as our saviour. We thought, why not play the creator?! Though it was more than a difficult task, with our team we did create deer in the system, and breathed life into their movements, real life kinetic movements!

THIS ONE is a project that exposed us to learning 350-year-old architecture techniques, and also a few that of the creator, so to say. Like I said everything about this project was larger than life and this includes the immense support, freedom and patience we enjoyed from the producer-director."

Fatima Meer - Narrative Vision

She is a highly respected Indian in South Africa, the country where she has made her home. She has worked with Shyam Benegal on *The Making of the Mahatma*, and feels passionate about Indian history. Working on the project for her became not only an obsession, but a mission as well, as it gave her an opportunity to dig into a chapter of Indian history that she had forgotten about.

Over a decade of research, of mulling over various references and interwoven stories, Fatima Meer has contributed immensely to what has finally been the story on screen.

"I MET Akbar and Marium Khan through a mutual friend, Uma Prakash, in 1997. I do not really know what inspired him to ask me to do the script. It may have been *The Making of the Mahatma*, for which I wrote the screenplay together with Shyam Benegal. I found him a very warm and attractive man. I was both happy and honoured at his request to write the script for his movie. He then sent me various research material. My first assignment to myself was to probe the story of the Taj Mahal. I found an incredible story. The family of Shahjehan and Mumtaz Mahal and the intense rivalry between the heir apparent, Dara Shikho and Aurangzeb, fascinated me. I delved into the characters and tried to give them a consistency throughout the plot, so that I would not have cardboard characters and a storyline that would be improbable, building the

characters and at every point questioning how each one would work in the situations they would find themselves in. This was in itself an exciting exercise. Working with Akbar Khan was wonderful. He added scenes, which at times I thought, breached the bounds of reality. But I soon realised that the flights of imagination he contributed enriched the screenplay. The last scene, in particular, where Shahjehan and Mumtaz Mahal meet again in the Taj Mahal after the death of the emperor is, to my mind, a flight of pure genius. One has only two-and-a-half to three hours to tell the story. I wish we had more time so that the sub-stories of Dara Shikho and his family could also have been brought into focus.

I DISCOVERED during my research the utterly intriguing Sarnad. Aurangzeb and his brother Dara bring into focus a modern conflict, that of between conservative Islam and liberal Islam, i.e. Sufism. Religious fundamentalism and liberalism, which happens to be such a burning issue today, was raised in the 14th century by Emperor Akbar and passed on to his great grandson Dara Shikho, who also translated the *Bhagvad Gita* into Urdu, and, thereby, opened it to international scrutiny through subsequent German and English translations. One might conjecture the course India would have taken post-14th century, if the rightful heir, Dara Shikho had succeeded the throne.”

“I was captivated by his passion and his total commitment to the film. He has sacrificed his all to bring this epic to life. I have not only come to admire the man, but also to love him.”

Akbar Khan - Producer

Born in an illustrious family of actor-film makers and businessmen, Akbar Khan went through all the rigors of the craft before launching himself in 1982 with a film called *Haadsa*. And though the much-appreciated film did not do very well at the box-office, it heralded the arrival of a sensitive actor and film maker.

Akbar Khan starred in a number of Hindi films before getting involved, for more than a decade, in mega television serials like *The Sword of Tipu Sultan* and *Akbar the Great*. But television was not his ambition, and the big screen always beckoned him. *Taj Mahal* thus became a major milestone in his life.

“I AM the only stupid producer, who could afford Akbar Khan as director. But when I looked around before embarking on this ambitious project, I found there was no one else I could hire, who would execute my dream — the dream of making a grand historical. Having made the choice of the director, I left him free in all creative matters and busied myself in making every resource possible to realise that dream. I stopped counting money. I believed in Akbar Khan's honesty, so I closed my eyes to his extravagances. I had worked with him earlier. He was just another actor waiting to be launched when I made *Haadsa* with him. Though it did not make money at the box- office, people still talk about it. I felt bad when he left my second venture, *Naam Hai Krishna*, mid-way to help his brother's television serial, *The Sword of Tipu Sultan*.

BUT HE more than made amends when we did the first multi-crore television serial, *Akbar the Great*, together. There was always a method in his extravagance. So, every penny has been well spent. The film has been shot in the most economical way possible, without compromising and without cutting costs, in two and a half years which is no joke when one looks at different aspects of the film's making — the costumes, the jewellery, the sets, the locations, the war sequences, the music, the song picturisations. I don't think as a producer I could have asked for more, and I am more than satisfied with the result. Thank you, Akbar Khan, for the wonderful job done. I now look forward to our next project together.”

Uttam Singh - Additional Notations

Uttam Singh started training in music at the age of four and has mastered the matka, tabla and the sitar. He entered the Mumbai film industry as a violinist, and soon started setting up music arrangement for different composers. His technical expertise shows through in the music compositions of films like *Maine Pyar Kiya* and *Hum Aapke Hain Kaun*.

Uttam Singh has scored independent music for blockbusters like *Dil To Pagal Hai*, *Dushman,* and *Gadar.* He has been associated with Naushad Ali as his music arranger for a long time.

Irshad Alam - Co-producer

A dynamic businessman who has taken his small family leather business to dizzy heights and gained international recognition as the leader of a reputed leather export house, in the city of Kanpur in Uttar Pradesh.

Irshad has always taken keen interest in Indian culture and its promotion. His foray into co-production has been a planned move. Investing in a film has been an extension of the desire and an exercise in promoting India across the globe.

AKBAR KHAN had always been fascinated by the glory of the Moghul Empire. The thirst for power, burning ambitions, intrigue, the rich heritage of art and culture and the fascinating personalities that were the building blocks of this empire. His foray into Moghul research began with *The Sword of Tipu Sultan.* The fascination continued with *Akbar the Great.* It was but natural that he would be interested in capturing the love story behind Taj Mahal on celluloid.

THERE WAS no question in his mind that he wanted to direct this film. It had all the trappings of a blockbuster. It was based on a true story, had love amidst a family feud and had the glory of a rich past. There is also the fact that there was a living witness to this tale - The Taj Mahal itself, a monument revered by lovers across the globe.

THE SIMPLEST decision was to make the film; then began chaos. How much of the story should be told? What should be left out? What is the fascination about the Taj Mahal beyond historical reverence? Questions but with very few answers. Akbar Khan nurtured this dream until it literally became an obsession that began to haunt him. The time spent on research just strengthened this and a detailed plan began to evolve. Fortunately for him, he managed to convince Fatima Meer into research. Here was someone who had the talent, the ability and the same passion to see the saga unfold on the big screen. Balancing between trying to tell a good story, to tell a credible story and yet remain honest to history was no easy task. Infact, it was formidable.

THIS BOOK seeks to record the experience of some of the artistes and technicians who were instrumental in helping Akbar Khan not only realise his dreams, but also make available an invaluable document to savour and enjoy for the future generation.

At the end of production, Akbar Khan heaved a sigh of satisfaction and said:

I can now understand how Shahjehan must have felt when he wanted to construct this tribute to his beloved wife. No comparisons, but judging from the sleepless nights that I have spent, I am sure his passion must have bordered on paranoia. I have spent a mere two years on my project, where Shahjehan spent almost twenty-two on his!!!

Rebuilding the monument - block by block

HERE IS the visual apology of the process of reconstruction. But its effect has to be seen on the big screen to be savoured, relished and retained in memory long after one makes a tearful exit from the cinema theatres.

I MET Akbar soon after he had finished the first edit of nearly the full film. At that time I had no idea that a book on the making of the film had been planned, and that somebody had tentatively been working on it or at least a figment or apology of it. Frankly, during the sneak preview one did not find many faults with the narrative pattern except, perhaps, the need to apply scissors here and there because once the main story began, the only loose ends were figments of one's imagination. One was convinced it was going to be another milestone in the history of motion picture making in India, certainly in the genre of historicals. The universal box-office response to the re-released *Mughal-e-Azam* was a clear indicator.

BUT IT seems during this particular screening (God alone knows how many times he must have run through the same sequences) Akbar detected a major flaw. What was Shahjehan doing when the mausoleum was being built? Certainly not just mourning alone for 22 years. I asked Akbar the question. Apparently, the emperor took keen interest in the construction of the monument from the conception and layout to final inlay work.